PRESENTED TO

_____

FROM

_____

FOREVER
SISTERS

CHERISHED MEMORIES & SIMPLE TRUTHS

D. A. MICHAELS

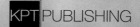

This is a book about sisters and the bonds that have been formed and proven over time. Maybe you are a sister to another sister, a sister to a brother, or a sister to someone not blood-related to you—whatever the makeup, you are a sister forever in their eyes, and they have written some of their thoughts about that treasured relationship—their *forever sister*.

Throughout this book you will read about relationship—connections that have occurred . . . not because you're fantastically unique—it is just because you are a sister.

Many stories are filled with emotion, while other pages are filled with simple quotes or inspiring thoughts allowing you an opportunity to share in the memories of your sister relationship.

The purpose of this book is to make you smile, cause you to remember, or simply allow you to see yourself within its pages. Perhaps it's been some time since you have spoken to your sibling and you need to reconnect. Maybe you have been wounded and you need to forgive . . . so you can heal.

We hope this book brings you that freedom—freedom to laugh, freedom to cry, freedom to enjoy life again with someone you love and who loves you.

Ecclesiastes 4:9-10 (NCV) reminds us of that simple truth:

> *"Two people are better than one,*
> > *because they get more done by working together.*
> *If one falls down,*
> > *the other can help him up.*
> *But it is bad for the person who is alone and falls,*
> > *because no one is there to help."*

So it is with sisters. You are not alone, someone is relying on you and you on them—you have been created to encourage and be encouraged. You are forever a sister, and not even time can change that truth.

May God bless your sister relationship! ✍ AD

Sister is probably the most

competitive relationship

within the family,

but once the sisters are grown,

it becomes the strongest relationship.

❋

MARGARET MEAD

Just so you know:
I love you more than life itself.
I couldn't ask for a better best friend.
You are one of the best people I know.
You are beautiful, always have been...
     people are finally catching on!

I look up to you.
You do great things and will forever!
          I luh you, I luh you, I luh you.

               XOXO,
                 D

JUST SO YOU KNOW:

LOVE YOU MORE THAN LIFE IT

COULDN'T ASK FOR A BETTER

M ARE ONE OF THE BEST PE

OU ARE BEAUTIFUL, ALWAYS.

CAT

I love my sister.

My older sister was rebellious and beautiful. When we hung out, I was never bored. I didn't get to hang out with her much growing up because we had different moms, but when she got her license we were inseparable. This December she will have been twenty-six. It's been seven years since she passed away, and I'd give anything to hug her one more time.

🌿 AC

GROWING UP, my world was as big

as my family's 160 acres and as small

as the five of us that lived on it.

Without a ruler to assess normality,

I always just assumed we measured up.

It was the childhood I knew,

the one I remember,

and the one I now treasure.

Because of my sisters.

Because We Are Sisters

The three of us girls piled into the mustard yellow—though officially it was harvest gold—1972 Chevy K5 Blazer. The backseat had long since been removed to make room for camping gear, hay bales, lumber, saddles, or junk, depending on the destination of the day, but the spare tire that lay loose in its place was plenty big enough for two kids to share. The third sister—or whoever had been lucky enough to call "Shotgun!"—claimed the passenger seat. Torn from top to bottom, with yellow foam oozing out the rupture, (pitted and gouged where little fingers couldn't resist the temptation to pluck away at it), the front seat itself was only a small step up from the spare tire.

From the driver's seat, Dad held sole jurisdiction over the myriad of buttons and dials, one of which controlled the radio and invited country music (was there any other kind?) to crackle through the speakers. Though the purpose of the other knobs was largely unknown to us, my curious baby finger held evidence that the glowing coil inside one of them functioned as a cigarette lighter.

From our perch on the spare tire, we watched the road go by beneath us through dime-sized holes in the exposed metal floor where the bolts anchoring the back seat used to be. We dropped tiny objects through the holes and looked out the back window to see if we could see them bouncing down the road. We were tone deaf and couldn't carry a tune between the three of us (at least that's what Dad said), but we sang "To the dump, to the dump, to the dump, dump, dump!" and whatever else came through the AM radio at the top of our lungs anyway. *Because we are sisters.*

The County dump wasn't a landfill site or a recycling station or even a sorting facility. It was simply the dump. It was only a few minutes from our home and was carved out of a small piece of farmland a few county roads over. As an unmanned facility, it was a veritable free-for-all for treasure hunting. My sisters and I practiced our balance-beam prowess and treaded carefully around the ledges of the concrete bins, scanning the contents hoping to find something worthy of a dumpster dive.

Landing new-to-us bicycles from the recesses of the rubbish pile was like winning the lottery. The two gold bikes with banana seats were too big for me, but the blue one with a red-and-white seat and shiny silver rivets was just my size. Souped-up with a new coat of paint and some accessories—spokey-dokes, handlebar streamers, and a bright orange flag—"new-to-us" was transformed into simply "new." We rode proudly down our gravel road and picked rocks out of one another's scraped knees when we would fall. *Because we are sisters.*

We abandoned the dump in the winter, and instead piled into the old Chevy to blaze a trail into the "back forty" to bring home the best Christmas tree we could find in the Deep Dark Forest—aptly named by three girls too scared to venture *there* alone. The three of us shared a room and feigned sleep each Christmas Eve after the annual reading of *'Twas the night before Christmas*, so we could tiptoe downstairs and sneak a peak at what was under the tree. Sometimes we even heard Santa on the roof, but we never let on. *Because we are sisters.*

There were no ice cream cakes or store-bought Halloween costumes at our house. Birthday cakes were baked by mom and sculpted into master pieces by dad, and if it could be fashioned from garbage bags—black or orange—and accessorized using bailing twine, sharpie pens, or poster board, we were it for Halloween. And when the other kids asked us what we were, we had one another's backs. *Because we are sisters.*

Our backyard play structure—forever referred to as "The Climbing Thing"—constructed entirely of two by fours, complete with fire pole, tireswing and slide, completed our " homemade" playground. It also consisted of a giant tractor tire painted white and filled with sand, in which we would build castles and pull the legs off of spiders; a parallel bar erected between two railroad tie posts, under which we would ride our pony and perform acrobatic feats; and black tires of various sizes (salvaged from the dump) buried halfway in the ground, perfect for leaping between and falling from. We picked one another up. *Because we are sisters.*

Deadfall trees were fashioned into a teepee in the yard, where we learned to ride our ponies bareback and jump on over their bums like the three amigos. We choreographed dance routines and performed them on the barn roof for imaginary audiences and raided the garden when we were hungry. We built log bridges across creeks, routinely overflowing our rubber boots. We pulled leaches off one another without batting an eye. *Because we are sisters.*

Normal was collecting giant rocks from the pasture and cracking them open with a hammer on the garage floor to see which ones had sparkles inside. Normal was digging up ant-hills until we found the one with the queen that headed up the homemade ant farm sandwiched between two pieces of glass. Normal was piling onto the motorcycle, three at a time, wrapping bare legs tightly around the gas tank as Dad did laps around our yard sending us into giggling hysterics while we squealed, "Yabba dabba doo time in Bedrock City!" Normal was spitting on the muffler afterwards just to delight in the sizzling sound it would make.

Today, the Blazer, now more rust-brown than harvest gold, sits parked outside because I can't bring myself to have it hauled away. Today, we sisters still consider it cheating to buy a ready-made costume from the store for Halloween. We sculpt birthday cake masterpieces for our kids and nieces and nephews, and try to channel The Deep Dark Forest as we browse through Christmas tree lots. On Christmas Eve, we sit down and read *'Twas the night before Christmas.* And sometimes we still hear Santa on the roof.

It has been a while since I pulled a bike out of that dump, performed a leach check, or spit on a muffler to hear it sizzle, but I can still feel the wind on my face, hear the squeals of my sisters, and taste the freedom of lapping that motorcycle around the yard. Three at a time. And I bet they can too.

Because we are sisters. ≥ NDF

I've always been very close to my sister.

To this day,

whenever she leaves

I break out into tears.

My Sister—My Best Friend

My sister is my best friend and is one of the people I trust the most in my life. We are four years apart, which seemed like a lot when we were younger. We were always dressed to match until I was around ten. I remember when we still shared a room together, she used to crawl in my bed because she was scared or we would just push our two beds together. I am now twenty-two and she will be eighteen years old in a few weeks—crazy how fast the time has gone by. I was her idol—still am to this day!

We have the best memories. I will never forget the nights we cried, laughed, and talked together or how much we giggling at the supper table while our parents sat clueless, wondering what was going on (we were usually kicking each other under the table). We still often stay up late just talking and listening to each other's stories, opinions, and feelings. Since we are still best friends, we go to parties together (she's the type of person that I am comfortable bringing around my friends).

I can't believe it, but she is graduating from high school at the end of the year, and I am incredibly proud of her accomplishments. She's on the student council, two cheerleading teams (soon to be three), and has tons of friends. After high school, she plans to become a cop, which makes me even more proud.

I love and respect the person she has become, and I will be there for her forever . . . no matter where life takes us. Even if she "ticked me off," I'm only a phone call away.

❧ BD

Sisters . . .
are for sharing laughter
and wiping tears.

Your sister isn't always
your blood relation,
sometimes she's that close friend
who understands you,
loves you,
and has always got your back
when you are in trouble.

❧

SISTER'S LOVE

She's my sibling, my sister,

a friend like no other

We're the product of love

between our father and mother

We may feud and fight,
    we don't always agree
But she'll watch my back
    and stand up for me
I'll stand by and support her,
    love and defend
There's no disagreement
    our love can't mend

It's a special connection

    this bond that we share

Sometimes it's capricious

    but it's always there

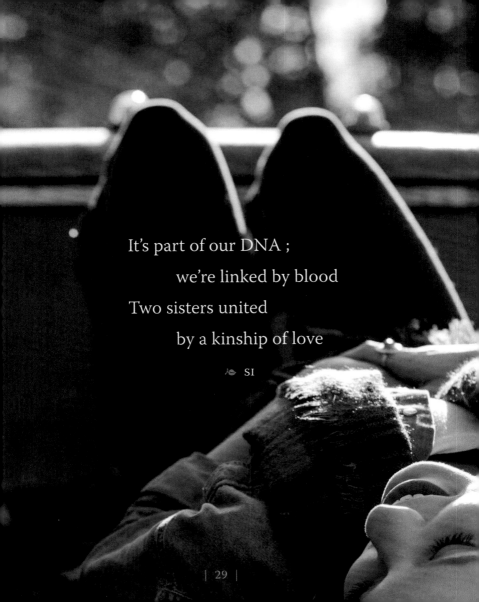

It's part of our DNA ;

we're linked by blood

Two sisters united

by a kinship of love

SI

We may have fought . . . maybe too much,
but I really did and do love my sister.
I still remember most of our
heart-to-heart conversations.

I wonder why we ever stopped . . .
time, new family relationships. I don't know.

I wished we could talk . . . like we used to.
It would be really good to talk to her.
I loved how my sister was there for me . . .
when I really needed her.

Today . . . I really need her.

I GREW UP in a little town on the prairies of South Dakota. I am the oldest of four with one brother and two sisters. When asked to share a family memory of mine, and this book is about sisters, I had one in mind, but asked my husband, "Can you think of any story from my childhood that I should share about one of my sisters?" Without hesitation he said, "The time you convinced your sister she was going to jail." Yep, that's the one I had thought of too. So whether it is printed or not, it feels good to confess.

JM :-)

"I don't want to go to jail!"

My parents were out of town and, being fifteen at the time and the oldest, I was in charge. The doorbell rang and shortly after my youngest sister told me that UPS had delivered a box for me and that she signed for it.

I asked, "Did you sign your name or mine?"

"Yours," she said.

I then proceeded to explain to her that signing for someone else is forgery, and she would, for sure, go to trial and probably spend a few years at the detention center a couple of towns over. She didn't believe me, which made me try harder, and so I went into great detail (and I mean great) about how tough things would be for her, how we would all miss her, but we could probably visit a couple of times a year.

She left the room, and about a half hour later, I couldn't find her. I looked all over the house, finally finding my sister buried in her bed under the covers sobbing her eyes out. I honestly didn't know why she would be crying and asked, "What's WRONG?"

She could hardly speak she was crying so hard, but managed to get out, "I don't want to go to jail!"

Well I was greatly relieved! *Easy one,* I thought. I assured her that I had been teasing and I was sorry, but I had only been joking around. She wasn't buying it.

"But I signed *your* name not mine and that is against the law!" I tried to reassure her but could not convince her otherwise.

So I said, "Come with me and we will go find the UPS man, and if HE tells you that you won't go to jail, will you believe him?"

"Sniff, sniff, yes."

So I grabbed my permit and off we went, driving up and down every street of our small town, looking, looking, and feeling more and more relieved as we weren't finding him.

"He probably is on to the next town, but next time he brings a box, I will ask him for you," I said and headed for home.

"There he is!" I heard from the back seat.

Sure enough, there he was, making a delivery at the local laundromat. So I parked the car, but was really thinking, *how in the world was I going to do this?*

I looked at my sister, whose face was beet red and swollen; the tears were still running down her cheeks. Then I looked at the UPS truck and tried to imagine telling the driver what the big problem was. He walked out from making his delivery, then I hopped out of the car.

"Excuse me," I said.

When he looked at me I felt like such a fool (my girlfriends and I all thought he was so cute, which only complicated the the situation), but some things you just have to do for your little sister when you are in charge and had created a huge mess.

Swallowing my teenage-crush awkwardness, I blurted out that he had delivered a box to our house, and my sister signed my name, and I told her that was forgery, and she would go to the detention center, and she believed me, and won't stop crying.

As I spoke, his eyes got bigger and bigger. Then he laughed pretty hard. *Ugh*. I felt like an even bigger fool! I asked if he would please go to our car and tell her she won't go to jail?

He opened the back car door and saw my little sister curled in a ball, doing those big, gulping, hiccough breaths you do when you have sobbed yourself sick, but he very kindly told her that she would NOT go to jail and that people sign for other people all the time.

She was instantly "healed" and gave him a huge smile. (And I do mean instantly. I still wonder about that instant smile.) I thanked him, and he laughed all the way to his truck and probably laughed the whole hour trip back to the warehouse, where he had a great story to share with his coworkers.

I did my best to avoid Mr. UPS after that incident. I would like to say I never teased anyone ever again, but that would be a lie. All that to say how thankful I am for both of my sisters.

My sisters and I have been through so much together. We have grown up together, have married, raised children who are now all grown and having children of their own. We went through the loss of our parents together. We have forgiven one another of all our childhood wrongs, and we are the best of friends. We laugh hardest when we are all together. I honestly can't imagine life without my two wonderful and—thankfully—forgiving sisters!

Sincerely, 🐟 JM

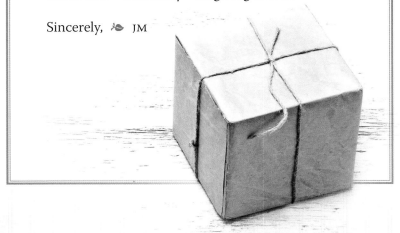

"There is no friend like a sister

in calm or stormy weather,

To *cheer* one on the tedious way,

to *fetch* one if one goes astray,

to *lift* one if one totters down,

to *strengthen* whilst one stands."

❁

CHRISTINA ROSSETTI

I remember . . .

        my sister had answers

        for everything.

She is my first and *only* lifeline.

Sisters are forever,

through thick and thin...

and sometimes deceit.

One of the many joys of having a sister are the memories we shared together: friends, our numerous "cutest-guy-in-home-room" talks, laughing until we couldn't breathe, secret sleepovers (when we'd sneak into one another's rooms at night without permission), and even the special winks and signals we developed. Then we grew up.

Many of those "sister" things remain between us, but many have changed—our viewpoints is one—especially when our own children came along. Then the rules Mom and Dad had for us didn't seem so silly and meaningless anymore. And now, as the aunt, we get to share in a different type of memory—sharing the wonderful stories of our nieces and nephews.

Before I share one of those stories, let me set the scenario: my middle sister has three daughters and a son. The two oldest are girls and are close in age. When they were little, both had snow-white blonde hair, one had straight hair, the other had what you would call "a riot of curls." Both beautiful and sweet, they would dance and sing, and both would say they were Lovely Linda—the Dancing Sister Brides.

With that in mind, it's hard for me to imagine them doing anything wrong—such sweethearts! And besides, my two sisters and I thought we were pretty good at anticipating things our kids might possibly get into. No one would ever pull the wool over our eyes, especially since we had all done some sneaking around ourselves and could spot the tricks a mile away, right? After my little sister's two oldest daughters were married (after our statute of limitations had run out), imagine our shock when the two "beauties" confessed something to my sister that my sisters and I would have never thought to do in a million years. And because they carried it off so seamlessly, we applaud them— enjoy our recollection of the event and a superb act of craftiness . . . at its best!

Operation: Obstacle Removal

One of the rules in our home growing up and passed along by my sisters and myself was that there was to be no watching of soap operas—NO exceptions. That was the rule and we obeyed.

My eldest niece, however, found a way around this rule. Her bedroom was downstairs, just off the family room where their TV and VCR were handily located. The problem was the TV was located in a place where if she watched it there, she would be heard and possibly found out.

So late at night, when everyone was asleep, she would sneak out to the family room, unhook the TV, unhook the VCR, carry them into her room and then rehook everything to watch her favorite soap (or the Backstreet Boys videos silently borrowed from a friend and safely tucked away above the drop ceiling in her room), unhook everything once again, carry them back to the family room, and replace everything as it was before.

One night she did cut herself in the process, leaving a scar that serves as a reminder of this sin in her life. *(Keep in mind, this was not in the day of the lightweight, flat screen TV! This was a big-ole, heavy TV set.)* She did this night after night, week after week. She must have been sort of thankful when the weekend rolled around and she could give her arms a break—and probably prepared her for carrying her own four children though—good, strong mom arms!

After some time her sister found out she was doing this, and rather than "tattling", she wanted in on the action, but her bedroom was upstairs, so what could they do? Sitting down together, they thought through some options—and BINGO! They found the fool-proof remedy. Their mom wanted them to practice the piano daily, and this was the perfect avenue through which they could carry out their plan.

That afternoon, they went to their mother with "a problem": they both needed to practice the piano for one hour per day, but those pesky younger siblings made it difficult, always interrupting and distracting them. They found it difficult to devote themselves fully to the development of their musical "gifts and talents"—which of course, they wanted to "use" in church. The plan: if mom would keep the younger two kids upstairs, this would give them a two-hour block each weekday to "practice."

Think about it: what mom wouldn't love to hear those words—going from forcing a child to practice to a willing heart, wanting to practice for an hour—each day.

So with the operation in full swing, my sister would diligently keep her younger two kids upstairs with the basement door closed, no doubt enjoying all the wonderful music floating up the stairs, never suspecting that her daughters were carrying out their plan; while one practiced (loudly), the other watched her favorite, forbidden daytime drama. It was easy as you please and no more hauling the TV and VCR back and forth.

Pure genius! MJ

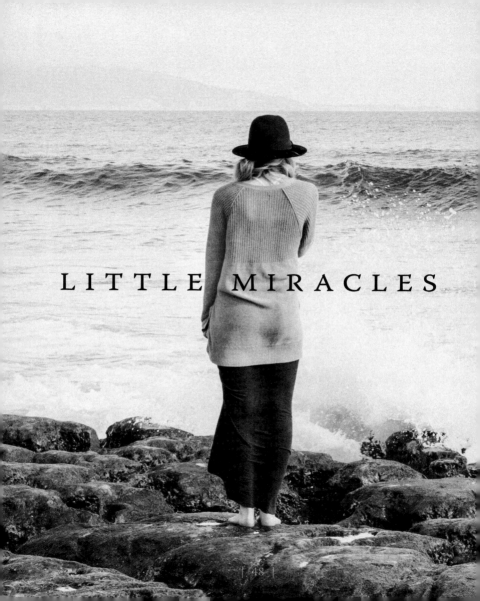

LITTLE MIRACLES

WHEN I WAS NINE my mom remarried. My brother and I had a new family, and soon, my mom announced that she was going to have a baby—a girl! I was going to be a new big sister!

I could not wait. So many of my friends had younger siblings, and I envied them. I would lie in bed at night dreaming of all we would do together, but especially I loved imagining what my little sister would look like—*just like me except with brown eyes and brown hair.*

Most of my prediction was correct (at least for a while), but soon her eyes changed color to bluish green. She's definitely more beautiful than I could have imagined, and even though she's much younger than me (eleven years), we're as close as sisters could be, which is probably what fueled our "mom"/best-friend relationship, but I would not want us any other way. I love her so much and have truly experienced the phrase:

> *Every time God closes a door,*
> *He truly does open a window.* ❧

Sister Mornings

I wasn't very kind to you much of the time,

but tried to make up for it by treating you

to little outings to show how much you mean to me.

I know brothers are supposed to be

nice to their sisters,

but I wish I had known how cool you were

and taken advantage of having you in more of my life.

I miss our morning donut runs.

You are married now… and live too far away.

DM

Wasted Years

My sister was born eight years after my parents were married. I'm sure they had begun to wonder if they would ever have children. She was a beautiful little girl with large brown eyes and dark hair, and the delight of all my parents' friends. She was very precocious and was happily ensconced as an adored little girl in a world of adults. Her world was turned upside down ten years later when I was born. To top it off, I was a twin—she now had two little sisters to compete with for the affection and attention of her parents.

Sadly my twin died at two months of age, and our mother was devastated. I later realized why our mother was so overprotective of me. She feared I might die too. My mother's attention and overprotection was interpreted by my sister as my being mother's favorite. This all must have been very hard for my big sister to understand and for me too. We had a wonderful mother, and she loved us both dearly and showed that love in many ways.

As many sisters do, we fought and fussed most of our lives, but I knew if I needed someone to talk to about my problems I could go to my big sister. Still, there was much contention between us.

Later, when she was diagnosed with a fatal kidney disease, I started spending more time with her. I took her to doctors' appointments, and we spent many hours talking about our early life. There was so much I didn't realize or know.

She told me about the day my twin died and how she was sent three blocks across town to fetch the doctor, since we did not have a phone. She ran as fast as she could and worried afterward that if she had only run faster, my twin might have lived. Of course that wasn't true, but to a ten-year-old it must have been a huge burden to bear.

After all the wasted years, we finally enjoyed a close and special relationship. Our dear mother was gone, and we didn't feel we had to compete for her affection—we had finally grown up.

She has passed away, but I feel so blessed to have had such a wonderful and talented sister. So many times I wish I could talk with her.

I miss her every day. ❧ SI

When I said,

"I won't tell anyone!"

sisters do

not count.

GROWING UP THE YOUNGEST in a family of four girls has its challenges. It seems everywhere I went, I was introduced as so-and-so's sister, and that moniker followed me throughout much of my younger years. Sure, there were times it had its perks, like having a few extra "inherited" friends, but mostly it came with a great deal of pressure to live up to and numerous expectations. Well, my story is not much different. Enjoy!

My Feet—Happy Feet

When I was in the fifth grade, I always thought my oldest sister looked so cool. The black "Doc Martin" combat boots were still trending, but she was the furthest thing from being "military." When I finally got the opportunity to buy a pair at a summer flea market, I wondered why mine didn't look so cool. Perhaps it was because they reminded me of something that Kirsten, one of the dolls from the American Girl collection, would have worn on the prairie, or perhaps it was just not *my* style after all. Years later, during a trip to England, I visited a *Doc Martin* store and bought a "genuine" pair of the black boots—but *they* were not *me*.

A few years later, at thirteen years old, I asked my second sister why she purchased a pair of eighty-dollar running shoes (they probably cost a lot more than that). She told me that as soon as I was running 5-8 miles per day, I could get some as well. For years I tried building my endurance so that I could buy some too, but I never did. More time passed, and eventually she was competing in her second Olympic games (yes, I said Olympics). I finally quit running, realizing that I just didn't like it. Running just was not me, so neither were the shoes.

Then, at age thirty-four, married and pregnant with our third child, our family traveled to celebrate my third sister's wedding reception. My soon-to-be-wed sister was able to go from workout shorts to a night out on the town without any bit of awkwardness, and the night of her reception was no exception. It was there that I saw another pair of shoes I wished to fit into—a bold orange pair of strappy heels. She was pure elegance in her form-fitting blue gown, and those heels that I imagined would look just as good on me. Keep in mind, I was the youngest and shortest in the family, but as much as I envisioned elegance, the truth is that heels

do wonders to give me that appearance of almost elegant. Funny how having three children to care for and squeezing my feet into soccer cleats for more than ten years, I could barely wear a two-inch wedge without my whole body aching the next day. I should have known.

My life has been fulfilling, yet discouraging, at times. Imagine you're being the youngest child, looking up to those you wish to be like—whose shoes you wish to fill, only to look down at your own feet, realizing how small they are. Having the smallest feet in the family, no one else's shoes fit me, and in time, I learned they were not meant to. I finally accepted that the only pairs of "shoes" that I should fit in were my own.

As much as I prefer being barefoot on a yoga mat, I still need to wear shoes from time to time. The amazing and beautiful thing, though, is that my shoes are just that—*mine*. There's no more pretending: these are my feet. There's no mistaking how I am fearfully and wonderfully created. I am designed with my own unique style, imagination, and life-path.

I have learned to choose wisely . . .

and the shoes I will fill.

RLR

forever sisters

© 2018 KPT Publishing, LLC
Written by D. A. Michaels

Published by KPT Publishing
Minneapolis, Minnesota 55406
www.KPTPublishing.com

ISBN 978-1-944833-30-5

Designed AbelerDesign.com

First printing April 2018

10 9 8 7 6 5 4 3 2 1

Printed in the United States of America